11+ English Spelling & Vocabulary

Intermediate Level
WORKBOOK 5

Dr Stephen C Curran
with Warren Vokes

Edited by Mark Schofield

This book belongs to

Accelerated Education Publications Ltd.

brighter	brightest	safer
safest	cooler	deeper
finer	miner	hiding
shining	smiling	hoping

Exercise 93a

1) They were warned not to __skate__ on the frozen lake as the ice was very thin.

2) It is much _____ to wait behind the motorway barrier if your car breaks down.

3) The ship had come to _____ on the rocks in the violent storm.

4) The diver descended still _____ into the dark depths of the sea.

5) The lights went out leaving the room in complete _____ .

6) The _____ pupils achieved excellent results in the examinations.

7) She could not help _____ when she thought of the joke he had told her.

8) The _____ reason for the poor result was his failure to revise.

9) "I was _____ that you would come and you didn't disappoint me."

10) She discovered the kitten _____ behind the sofa.

Score /10

Exercise 93b

11) It was a cloudless evening and the moon was _____ brightly in the night sky.

12) "We're all going _____ at the local ice rink. Would you like to come too?"

13) The rain clouds had passed over and the sky was looking much _____ .

14) Caster sugar is much _____ than granulated sugar.

15) He suffered from a very serious _____ but now he is fully recovered.

16) The _____ way to cross a busy road is to use the pelican crossing.

17) It was a very hot day but much _____ in the shade under the tree.

18) She had seen the _____ steal the handbag and gave a statement to the police.

19) His father had been a _____ and now he too worked down the pit.

20) Their skin had been _____ by the sun's ultra violet rays.

Score /10

2

© 2006 Stephen Curran

Word Bank

skate, skating, darkness, illness, chief, thief, grief, burnt

Word Bank TOTAL 1,860

Across 93

1. Giving out light.
4. Bottom-dwelling marine fish with a flattened body.
7. Somebody who steals.
8. Giving off stronger light.
10. A disease or sickness.
13. The absence of light.
15. Lower in pitch.
16. The person with the most authority in a group.
17. Great sadness.
18. Least likely to cause harm.

Put the mystery letter (✸) into the box marked **93** below. Add in the mystery letters from puzzles **94** to **100** then rearrange them to make **Dickens's Mystery Word**.

The clue is **TREE**.

Down

2. Wishing something to be true.
3. Sliding along a slippery surface.
5. Less coarse.
6. Reflecting the strongest light.
8. Destroyed by fire.
9. Concealing from view.
11. Making a pleasant expression.
12. Someone who digs underground for coal.
14. Less likely to result in injury or damage.
16. Colder, but usually pleasantly so.

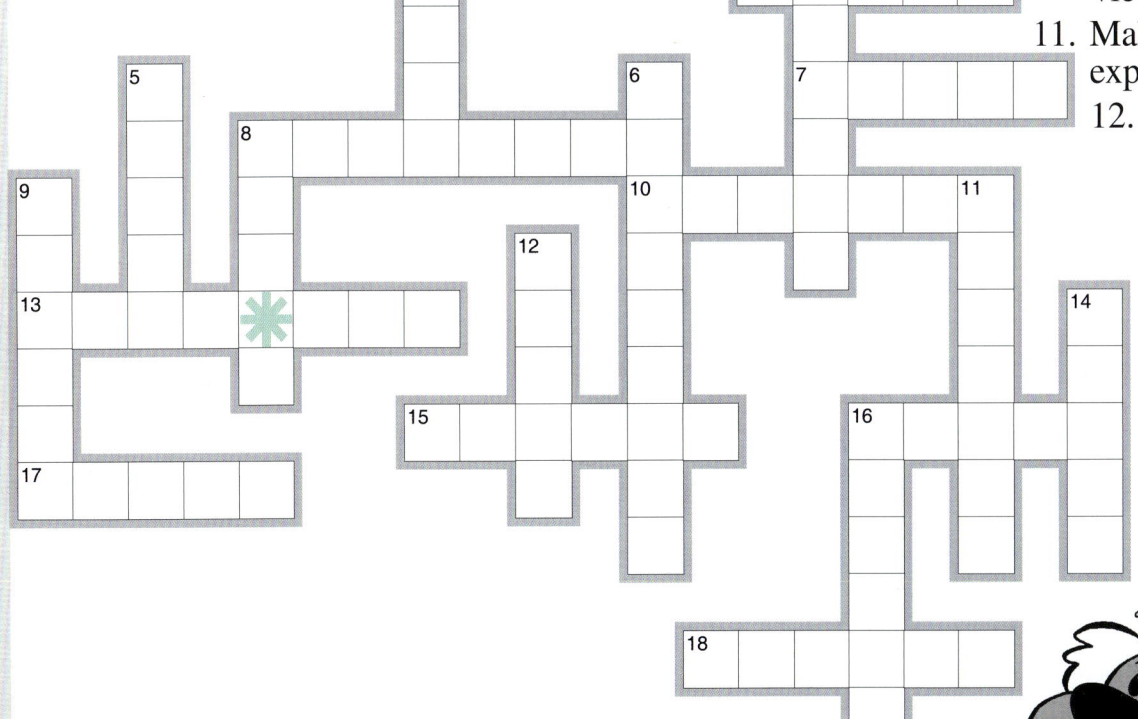

93 94 95 96 97 98 99 100

Enter your mystery letters here:

Now rearrange them:

Mystery Word:

Score /20

© 2006 Stephen Curran

should cheer quickly
nearly write writing
wrote wrap prove
move remove repeat

Across

1. Words written down.
5. Modelling substance.
7. To coil around something.
10. Christian festival commemorating the resurrection of Jesus Christ.
12. To change position.
13. Almost but not quite.
15. Somebody who writes poems.
18. To make a casual comment or observation.
19. To take away something.

94

Down

2. Fix or mend something.
3. Having the colour of ash or lead.
4. Christian festival celebrating the birth of Jesus Christ.
6. Moving or doing something fast.
7. Composed and sent a letter.
8. A piece written in verse.
9. Establish the truth or existence of something.
11. To be scheduled or expected to be.
14. Say something again.
16. Put words on paper.
17. Shout of approval.

Mystery Letter

Score 20

4 © 2006 Stephen Curran

grey **clay**
poem **poet**
remark **repair**
Easter **Christmas**

Exercise 94a

1) At _____ we were given lots of chocolate eggs.

2) William Wordsworth, the famous English _____ , wrote *The Daffodils*.

3) John _____ home to his parents every week while away at boarding school.

4) She was rushing in the heavy traffic and _____ had an accident.

5) "I will say the phrase once, then you _____ it after me."

6) The potter threw another lump of _____ onto the wheel and began again.

7) If you wish to stay healthy you _____ take lots of exercise.

8) I asked the jeweller if he could _____ the broken clasp on my bracelet.

9) I always attend midnight Mass on _____ Eve.

10) She managed to _____ the splinter from his finger.   Score ⎕/10

Exercise 94b

11) She recited the _____ which she had written especially for the occasion.

12) "Come _____ , they are showing the rocket launch on television right now."

13) The ability to read and _____ are two basic skills that everyone should learn.

14) They suspected he was guilty but they could not _____ it.

15) It was only a casual, off-the-cuff _____ but it caused great offence.

16) J. K. Rowling is famous the world over for _____ the *Harry Potter* books.

17) When he won, a huge _____ from his supporters echoed round the stadium.

18) He found some pretty paper with which to _____ her birthday present.

19) For his interview he wore a neutral-coloured dark _____ suit.

20) "It's your turn: shake the dice and _____ your counter."   Score ⎕/10

© 2006 Stephen Curran

aloud	around	alike
afraid	coal	roast
cloak	float	yesterday
afternoon	however	breakfast

Exercise 95a

1) She was a _____ now that her daughter had given birth to a son.

2) Every morning he ate _____ before going to school.

3) A new _____ of his favourite bookshop opened in the town.

4) Today is Tuesday, so the day before _____ was Sunday.

5) "We need some more _____ for the fire: could you refill the scuttle?"

6) I ordered a fruit sundae and my mum had a _____ Melba.

7) It's not often you see a _____ chestnut vendor on the street.

8) He turned the car _____ and headed back the way he had come.

9) Although he sometimes took the bus, it was more _____ for him to cycle.

10) "We thought we'd lost you. _____ did you find us?"

Score /10

Exercise 95b

11) In the storm several _____ had been ripped from the trees.

12) "Meet me for lunch at one o'clock tomorrow _____ ."

13) He increased the length of line beneath the _____ to fish nearer to the bottom.

14) "I'm _____ she won't be in today - can I take a message?"

15) Cattle and wild ponies are allowed to _____ throughout the New Forest.

16) She stood in front of the class and read _____ a passage from the book.

17) He could just hear their shouts _____ the roar of the water rushing past.

18) He opened a tin of _____ , drained off the syrup and put them in a dish.

19) She threw her _____ over her shoulders and fastened the frog.

20) The twins were so _____ they were almost identical.

Score /10

roam   grandmother
above   usual
branch   branches
peach   peaches

Word Bank TOTAL 1,900

Across   95   ## Down

1. Part of a tree growing from the trunk.
4. Normal, customary or typical.
5. On all sides of or somewhere near.
7. A loose, sleeveless outer garment.
9. Sweet, round, juicy fruits with a stone.
12. The mother of your father or mother.
15. Rest on the surface of a liquid.
16. Frightened.
17. First meal of the day.
19. Local units of an organisation.
20. The day before this one.

2. Using an audible speaking voice.
3. In whatever way or to whatever degree.
6. Creamy orange colour tinged with yellow.
8. Similar in appearance.
10. Daytime between noon and evening.
11. Black rock used as fuel.
13. Directly overhead.
14. To wander aimlessly.
18. Oven-cooked meat.

Mystery Letter   Score /20

© 2006 Stephen Curran

classes   glasses   order
border   together towards
afterwards forward inches
worth   starve   husband

Across

2. A woman's spouse.
8. In company with others in a group.
12. Weaken or die through hunger.
13. In a particular direction.
14. A hot condiment.
15. Fill by pushing things into it.
17. Periods of teaching.
18. At a later time than that mentioned previously.

Down

1. Moves by small degrees.
3. Two times.
4. Towards the front.
5. Instruction to do something.
6. Outer eyewear.
7. Subsequently or because.
9. A band running along the edge.
10. Large pot used to boil water.
11. Something's monetary value.
14. Cost of something bought or sold.
16. Enclosing structure usually made of wood.
17. End of the sleeve nearest the wrist.

Mystery Letter

Score /20

© 2006 Stephen Curran

price **twice**
since **fence**
pepper **copper**
cuff **stuff**

Exercise 96a

1) All she had to do then was to _____ the turkey and wrap it in cooking foil.

2) There were three _____ : one for white wine; one for red; and one for water.

3) The bride and her new _____ posed with their families for photographs.

4) They checked the compass bearing and set off _____ the far hill.

5) "If you all move _____ a little, we can get more people in behind you."

6) They travelled south through Texas and crossed the _____ into Mexico.

7) The torch flashed _____ and then once again. Three flashes, that was the signal.

8) Last weekend my dad and our neighbour replaced the garden _____ .

9) As he went to shake my hand, I noticed that his shirt _____ was frayed.

10) _____ is an excellent conductor of electricity and heat.

Score /10

Exercise 96b

11) The car collection at Beaulieu must be _____ millions of pounds.

12) They walked _____ , hand in hand, along the towpath.

13) They saw the show and _____ had a meal in a nearby restaurant.

14) Dancing _____ were held in the church hall and Lucy wanted to enrol.

15) The two cars narrowly avoided a collision and missed by only a few _____ .

16) He never used the salt from the cruet but he liked lots of _____ .

17) The crops have failed due to the drought and many people could _____ .

18) We were at school together but we have not seen each other _____ then.

19) In the library all the books are in alphabetical _____ by author.

20) "I bought it in the sale at a greatly reduced _____ ."

Score /10

© 2006 Stephen Curran

visit	fir	birth
birthday	bitter	silly
stiff	hurry	provide
pretend	forest	track

Exercise 97a

1) It was so _____ that you could hear a pin drop.

2) They sent out many cards to announce the _____ of their second child.

3) The menu in the Chinese restaurant listed a huge variety of _____ .

4) He asked the manufacturer to _____ a list of spare parts.

5) Following the narrow _____ through the woods, they came to a clearing.

6) The dense _____ of conifer trees was being grown for paper production.

7) He asked his closest _____ to be the best man at his wedding.

8) When they were all _____ the instructor began the training.

9) She was driving so she ordered a non-alcoholic drink of _____ lemon.

10) A collection of _____ cones was on display on the nature table.

Score /10

Exercise 97b

11) It is her thirteenth _____ and she is now a teenager.

12) The overnight frost had frozen the washing on the line and made it _____ .

13) The little boy would _____ he had a playmate when he played on his own.

14) A slice of _____ is often added to tea instead of milk or sugar.

15) Simon had a sweet tooth and covered his cereal with far too much _____ .

16) When her father was in hospital, Victoria would _____ him every evening.

17) His job was to make up and fill the _____ , then seal the lids with vinyl tape.

18) The old document showed that his family used to _____ in the little cottage.

19) It was a _____ thing to have done and now he felt very foolish.

20) "_____ up, we're going to miss the train!"

Score /10

© 2006 Stephen Curran

Word Bank

dwell present
lemon sugar
friend quiet
boxes dishes

Word Bank TOTAL 1,940

97

Across

6. Making little or no noise.
7. In a particular place.
8. Somebody emotionally close to another.
11. Make available.
12. Evergreen tree with needle-shaped leaves.
14. Containers for serving food.
15. Ridiculous.
17. Event of being born.
18. Mark left by a moving person, animal or thing.

Down

1. Fights using fists.
2. Day somebody is born.
3. Go to see someone.
4. White or brown sweet-tasting substance.
5. Rigid, inflexible or hard to move.
8. Large dense growth of trees.
9. Reside.
10. Rush or speed up.
11. To make believe.
13. Strong and sharp in taste.
16. Yellow or green citrus fruit.

Mystery Letter   Score /20

© 2006 Stephen Curran

finger   flesh   wool
bloom   cling   strip
pint   gift   serve
person   term   upset

Across

3. Hold tightly with hands or arms.
5. An individual human being.
7. Sheep's short curly hair.
10. Team of 11 players, for example a football, hockey or cricket team.
12. A bouncing cricket shot to the boundary.
13. Soft tissue of the body.
15. Overturned or spilled.
16. A musical interval equal to an octave plus a third.
18. Digit of the hand.
19. A special talent or skill that someone appears to be have been born with.

Down

1. To open into flower.
2. Easy to do, understand or work out.
4. To put a ball or shuttlecock in play.
6. The number 12.
8. Division of an academic year.
9. Remove old paint or varnish.
11. Item number five in a series.
12. One of four equal parts.
14. The digit three places to the left of the decimal point.
17. Unit of liquid measurement.

98

four   fourth
fifth tenth
eleven simple
twelve hundred

Exercise 98a

1) The United States celebrates Independence Day on the _____ of July.

2) The football team only had ten players and needed one more to make _____ .

3) The runway at Nice airport is just a _____ of land built offshore.

4) The instructions were _____ and easy to follow.

5) His new shoes were rubbing, so he put some sheep's _____ inside his sock.

6) His first four shots failed to hit the target but his _____ was a bull's eye.

7) The _____ was an ace and unplayable by her opponent.

8) There are one _____ cents in one Euro.

9) She was very _____ and her friend tried to console her.

10) He could not remember the _____ and final commandment.

Score /10

Exercise 98b

11) It was the end of the school _____ and now they had three weeks' holiday.

12) The small child was still afraid and continued to _____ tightly to his mother.

13) He cut his _____ opening the tin and needed a plaster to stop the bleeding.

14) The dog had not eaten for days and had little _____ on his bones.

15) It was her last day at the firm and her workmates bought her a small _____ .

16) Christine put the custard powder into the _____ jug and added boiling water.

17) "The _____ who did this has upset the whole class and should be ashamed."

18) A square, rectangle, trapezium, rhombus and rhomboid all have _____ sides.

19) The flowers at the horticultural show were all in full _____ .

20) The _____ disciples joined Jesus for the Last Supper.

Score /10

© 2006 Stephen Curran

daisy   daisies   lily
lilies   wise   spider
soap   soak   earn
earth   grace   space

Exercise 99a

1) Climbing the _____ slope was difficult, especially carrying heavy rucksacks.

2) He ran out of _____ and could not fit any more CDs into the rack.

3) After exercising, she liked to _____ in a hot bath for fifteen minutes.

4) He watched the _____ spinning its web and was fascinated by the process.

5) He had a puncture and had to change the _____ at the roadside.

6) The drought had lasted many weeks and the _____ was dry and cracked.

7) A frog sat on the large, flat leaf of a water _____ .

8) Although he was very tired and sore, he ran on _____ and finished the race.

9) She was not sure but she took a _____ and guessed the answer correctly.

10) It was a very brave _____ and he was awarded a medal.

Score / 10

Exercise 99b

11) The padlock was made from hardened _____ and was extremely strong.

12) Sean had a clear soprano _____ and sang in the school choir.

13) Anna worked on Saturdays to _____ some extra pocket money.

14) The old man had lived a full and varied life and was very _____ .

15) She planned to _____ all her friends to her summer barbecue.

16) She taught her young son to wash his hands with _____ and hot water.

17) "Sit here on the grass and I'll show you all how to make a _____ chain."

18) They picked the _____ and strung them together by slitting their stems.

19) On top of the coffin was a wreath of white _____ from his wife.

20) He asked the minister to say _____ before the meal.

Score / 10

Word Bank

voice, invite, steep, wheel, bravely, chance, steel, deed

Word Bank TOTAL 1,980

99

Across

2. To move quickly in a circle.
4. Plant with short stems and flowers with white or pinkish-white petals.
6. Cleansing agent.
11. Soft, workable material in which plants grow.
13. Sound made by using vocal organs.
14. Make money by working.
15. Strong alloy of iron and carbon.
16. Knowing much from experience.
17. Make something or somebody completely wet.
18. A prayer at mealtimes.

Down

1. An intentional act.
3. Perennial plant that has layered bulbs, blade-shaped leaves and single large flowers.

Down (continued)

5. To set things some distance apart.
6. An arachnid that spins webs.
7. Plural of 3 Down.
8. The likelihood that something will happen.
9. Acting in a manner showing courage when faced with danger, difficulty or pain.
10. To ask to participate.
12. Tall plants that have flowers with white petals radiating from a round yellow centre.
15. To soak something in a liquid, especially for cleaning or softening or to extract something.

Mystery Letter

Score /20

© 2006 Stephen Curran

thirteen	fourteen	fifteen
sixteen	thirty	twenty
fifty	sixty	thousand
creeping	indeed	between

Exercise 100a

1) The _____ Years' War was fought in Europe between 1618 and 1648.

2) Four score (four times _____) equals eighty.

3) Jesus fed the five _____ with five loaves and two fishes.

4) He broke the _____ and distributed them among those present.

5) Only a few metres remained _____ him and the winning post.

6) She divided the chewy bar into two equal _____ and gave the boys one each.

7) The _____ made off on foot with the stolen goods.

8) He arrived at eight forty-five: _____ minutes before the nine o'clock meeting.

9) The tide was coming in and the sea was _____ slowly up the beach.

10) She retired at the age of _____ and drew her pension.

Score 10

Exercise 100b

11) Many superstitious people consider the number _____ to be unlucky.

12) At _____ she was old enough to learn to ride a motor scooter.

13) "Would you prefer a brown _____ or a white one?"

14) The new-born _____ was suckling milk from its mother's udder.

15) It cost £48.50. He paid with a _____ pound note and received £1.50 in change.

16) The _____ was too high for her to reach, so she fetched some steps.

17) She had eaten six of the twenty sweets and now there were only _____ left.

18) "He's not a very good eater and often _____ half his meal untouched."

19) "I expect the _____ he does eat is enough for him."

20) He was very keen, _____ eager, to have a go himself.

Score 10

16 © 2006 Stephen Curran

half calf
shelf loaf
halves leaves
thieves loaves

Word Bank TOTAL 2,000

Across 100

2. Fourth digit to the left of the decimal point.
5. Group of 14 objects.
6. Young cow or bull.
14. Steals.
15. A score of things.
16. Number 50.
17. From one place to another.
18. Number 13.

Down

1. What is more.
3. Number 60.
4. Spend time lazily.
5. A team of 15 players, especially a rugby union team.
6. Developing or advancing gradually over a period of time.
7. Quantities of bread shaped and baked as a whole.

Down (continued)

8. Score in tennis awarded to the player with a score of fifteen on winning another point.
9. A ledge of rock, sand, or ice.
10. Something with a value of 16.
11. Hinged or removable sections of a table top.
12. Two equal periods of play into which some games are divided.
13. One of two equal parts.

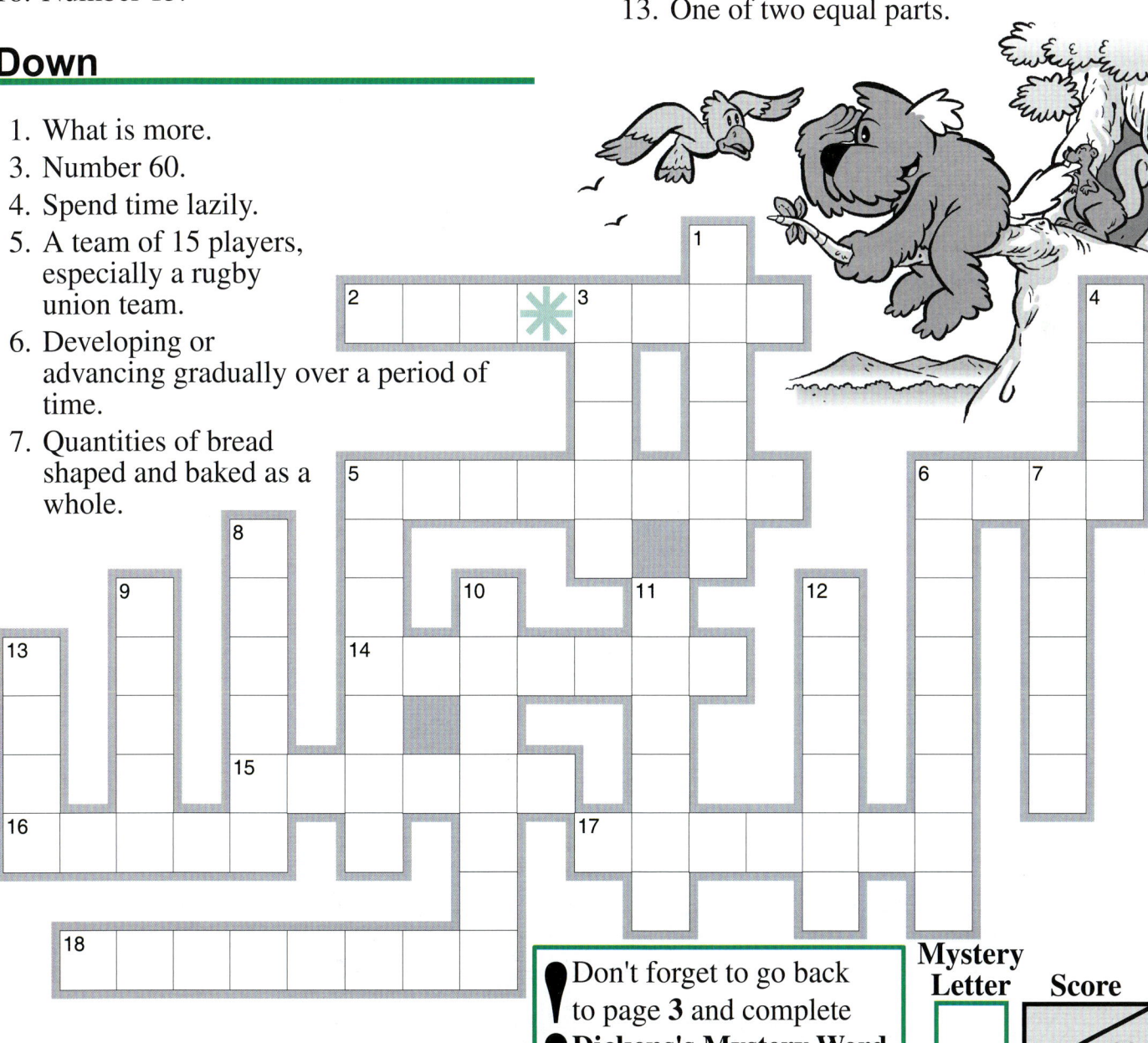

! Don't forget to go back to page 3 and complete
● Dickens's Mystery Word.

Mystery Letter

Score /20

© 2006 Stephen Curran

In the Living Room

Can you find all these words in the picture below? Write the correct word against each number.

settee	armchair	vase	newspaper	television
bookcase	mantelpiece	plant	plug	speaker
cushion	magazine	hearth	pen	candle

1. _____ 2. _____ 3. _____
4. _____ 5. _____ 6. _____
7. _____ 8. _____ 9. _____
10. _____ 11. _____ 12. _____
13. _____ 14. _____ 15. _____

18 © 2006 Stephen Curran

In the Bathroom

Can you find all these words in the picture below? Write the correct word against each number. When you have finished you can colour in the picture if you want to.

scales	wash basin	shower	toothpaste	razor
cistern	toothbrush	water	taps	pedestal
shower gel	mat	towel	toilet	soap

1._____ 2._____ 3._____

4._____ 5._____ 6._____

7._____ 8._____ 9._____

10._____ 11._____ 12._____

13._____ 14._____ 15._____

© 2006 Stephen Curran

flew	threw	crew
chew	wolf	themselves
grind	thrown	knee
kneel	knot	knock

Exercise 101a

1) He could escape if he could just manage to untie the _____ in the rope.

2) It was an error of judgement and they had only _____ to blame.

3) He had asked the builder to repair it but still it had not been _____ .

4) The aircraft refuelled at Singapore and then _____ on to Australia.

5) Her horse stopped abruptly at the hurdle and she was _____ from the saddle.

6) She sent off for a new set of kitchen _____ that she saw in an advertisement.

7) The _____ of the *Enola Gay* dropped the atom bomb on Hiroshima.

8) He would always _____ his food thoroughly to help his digestion.

9) "Don't _____ down your food, you'll get indigestion!"

10) He was kept in _____ overnight and questioned next morning.

Score 10

Exercise 101b

11) The old man's progress along the corridor was _____ - paced and painfully slow.

12) While the men went to watch the game, their _____ went shopping.

13) "I put it in the _____ last week, so it should have been delivered by now."

14) The bell seemed not to be working, so he gave a loud _____ on the door.

15) "Would the boys at the very front _____ down for the photograph."

16) He had an operation on his _____ to repair the patella.

17) He _____ the ball in from the boundary and the wicket-keeper caught it.

18) The _____ was broken and the express train left the track at high speed.

19) My dad uses an electric carving _____ for the roast joint on Sunday.

20) Her husband would _____ his teeth while he slept.

Score 10

Word Bank

knife, wives, mail, snail, knives, fixed, rail, jail

TOTAL 2,020

101

Across

1. Tool for cutting or spreading.
4. To hit repeatedly.
5. To pulverise something.
6. Past participle of *'throw'*.
7. Plural of *'wife'*.
10. Their normal selves.
12. Place where criminals are kept.
13. Securely in position.
15. Travelled on an aircraft.
16. Long length of wood or metal to hang things from.
17. Gnaw something repeatedly.

Down

1. Way of tying a length of rope, string, thread, or other material.
2. Tools with a sharp blade and a handle.
3. To rest on, or get down on, one or both knees.
4. Middle joint of the human leg.
8. Gastropod with a coiled shell and a retractable muscular foot.
9. Carnivore that hunts in packs.
10. Past tense of *'throw'*.
11. Items sent in a postal system.
14. Ship's staff excluding officers.

Put the mystery letters from the starred squares (✳) from puzzles **101** to **107** into their numbered box below, then rearrange them to make **Kate's Mystery Word**. The clue is **FRUIT**.

Enter your mystery letters:

101 102 103 104 105 106 107

Now rearrange them to make the:

Mystery Word:

© 2006 Stephen Curran

flock   finish   tie
tied   raise   raised
trunk   strike   cure
sure   pure   picture

Across

2. Take somebody prisoner.
6. Group of birds or sheep.
10. Perfect dwelling place after death.
11. Unquestioningly true or real.
12. On the point of death.
13. To restore a sick animal or person to health.
15. To feel extremely frightened or worried about something that may happen in the future.
17. To come to, or bring something to an end.
18. Not mixed with any other substance.
19. Completely or partially unable to hear in one or both ears.
20. Given money in return for work.

Down

1. An equal score or result in a game, race or competition.
3. Something drawn or painted.
4. To act as a parent or guardian to somebody while he or she is growing up.
5. Large travelling case.
7. Deliberately saying something untrue.
8. Made a knot.
9. Moved something to a higher level.
14. To stop working as a protest.
16. Protect somebody or something from attack, harm, or danger.

102

Mystery Letter

Score

20

© 2006 Stephen Curran

capture	defend
dying	lying
dread	deaf
heaven	paid

Exercise 102a

1) The animal was very sick and was clearly _____ of the disease.

2) He saw the older boy _____ the younger one, who then fell to the ground.

3) She showed her art teacher the _____ that she had painted.

4) He was profoundly _____ in both ears and had not heard the bus approaching.

5) Teams of experts finally managed to _____ the *Mary Rose* from the sea bed.

6) "You have five minutes left to _____ the test."

7) He _____ his entrance money at the kiosk and went into the exhibition.

8) He thought he would be able to do it easily but now he was not so _____ .

9) They all stood and _____ their glasses for the loyal toast.

10) The condition was terminal with no known _____ .

Score ___ / 10

Exercise 102b

11) "This place would be _____ , if it weren't for the people that live here!"

12) They managed to _____ two enemy soldiers for interrogation.

13) The elephant extended its _____ towards them and sniffed loudly.

14) She used to _____ Mondays because the first lesson was double maths.

15) "I know you are _____ , Tomkins. Tell me the truth and I will not punish you."

16) The shepherd tended his _____ of sheep and brought them down from the hills.

17) He bent down to _____ his shoelace and the man behind walked into him.

18) The spring water was clear and tasted very _____ .

19) The soldiers tried to _____ their position but they were overrun.

20) The match was _____ with three goals each.

Score ___ / 10

© 2006 Stephen Curran

built	build	building
content	battle	rattle
cattle	tired	kettle
bottle	cork	sore

Exercise 103a

1) "Put the _____ on and we'll have a nice cup of tea."

2) We watched the dolphins _____ ahead of the ship's bow.

3) Trafalgar was a very intense naval _____ with many casualties on both sides.

4) The critics did not _____ the film very highly but I enjoyed it immensely.

5) He was very arrogant and his _____ was very condescending.

6) "The castle's haunted and sometimes you can hear the _____ of chains."

7) He _____ the house himself and it took him nearly four years to complete.

8) She took the painting to an art gallery and asked them to _____ it for her.

9) No _____ how hard she tried, she could not follow the knitting pattern.

10) He slowed the car down to cross the _____ grid.

Score / 10

Exercise 103b

11) He used a penknife to _____ the dried mud off his shoes.

12) The milkman had dropped a _____ and there was milk all over the pavement.

13) The roof and windows of the old _____ needed much restoration.

14) Never _____ to leave work for others, she always offered to help.

15) Coming down the wet stairs too quickly, she _____ and sprained her ankle.

16) His skin was very _____ with sunburn and the bedcovers aggravated the pain.

17) The Olympic _____ was carried across the country by a series of runners.

18) He pulled the _____ from the bottle and poured them both a glass of wine.

19) She was so _____ she could hardly keep her eyes open.

20) It was a close match and the tension began to _____ .

Score / 10

24 © 2006 Stephen Curran

rate	flame
frame	scrape
swimming	slipped
matter	manner

Word Bank TOTAL 2,060

103

Across

7. Quite satisfied and happy.
8. To move something hard, sharp, or rough across a surface.
9. A surrounding structure.
10. To set a value on something.
11. Cylindrical piece of material used as a bottle stopper.
13. Made a structure by fitting the parts of it together.
14. A structure with walls and a roof.
15. Slid out of the proper or desired position.
16. Container for boiling water.
17. A painful open skin infection or wound.

Down

1. To preserve fruit or vegetables in a glass container.
2. The way in which something is done or happens.
3. Needing rest.
4. A substance or material of a particular kind.
5. Moving unsupported through the water using the arms and legs.
6. Hot glowing body of burning gas.
10. To make somebody lose his or her composure.
11. Farm animals of the ox family.
12. The physical structure, shape and size of a person.
13. A large-scale fight between armed forces.

Mystery Letter

Score /20

© 2006 Stephen Curran

toe scout shout
axe trying flying
army rank shy
spy butterfly answer

Across

104

2. Large armed fighting force.
5. Without difficulty or strain.
6. To engage in espionage.
7. Utter something very loudly.
10. High status.
11. Armed conflict between countries.
13. A digit of the foot.
14. Response to a question.
15. Uncomfortable in the company of others.
19. Even less difficult.
20. Insect with two pairs of brightly coloured wings.

Down

1. Lively and cheerfully.
3. Happening or passing very quickly.
4. The superlative of 'easy'.
8. Weighing the most.
9. Placing great strain on somebody's patience, composure, or good nature.
12. Weighing a lot.
16. Weighing even more.
17. To cut something, for example expenditures or services, drastically.
18. To gather information about an enemy's position.

Mystery Letter

Score

20

26 © 2006 Stephen Curran

heavy   heavier
heaviest   war
easier   easiest
easily   merrily

Word Bank TOTAL 2,080

Exercise 104a

1) It is _____ to climb up a ladder than it is to climb down.

2) The Red Admiral _____ is found in Europe and North America.

3) The bucket was very _____ when it was filled with water.

4) Mary spent the whole evening _____ to finish her homework.

5) "Don't be _____ , come in and meet everyone."

6) The forestry worker used an _____ to fell the tree.

7) There were three routes up the mountain and they chose the _____ .

8) The captain announced, "We shall be _____ at an altitude of 28,000 feet".

9) She left the _____ of the four bags for her husband to carry.

10) He was a _____ during the war and was tried for treason.

Score /10

Exercise 104b

11) The parcel weighed 18kg and was _____ than the 15kg maximum limit.

12) The police sergeant was promoted to the _____ of inspector.

13) He was walking round the house barefoot and stubbed his _____ on the table leg.

14) "There's no need to _____ , I'm not deaf!"

15) The children were laughing and playing _____ with each other.

16) The English Civil _____ began in 1642 and lasted for two years.

17) Looking through the telescope he could _____ read the name on the ship's stern.

18) An _____ of volunteers cleared the litter and tidied the river bank.

19) The _____ Association was founded in 1908 by Lord Baden-Powell.

20) "The phone's ringing, could you _____ it for me please."

Score /10

© 2006 Stephen Curran

cause	because	instant
shadow	arch	starch
touch	being	past
mast	fasten	odd

Exercise 105a

1) The sailor climbed up the ship's _____ to the crow's nest.

2) The vase shattered the _____ it hit the floor.

3) Her parents waved _____ from the station platform as the train departed.

4) He sent the letter and kept a _____ of it for himself.

5) "Please _____ your seat belts, the aeroplane is about to take off."

6) At the laundry, they used too much _____ and the hotel sheets were very stiff.

7) The waiter poured the wine and waited for his customer to _____ it.

8) They passed through the _____ and out onto the road.

9) "I'm afraid I can't help you _____ we have no spare parts in stock."

10) She was rushing and, in her _____ , she crashed the car.

Score / 10

Exercise 105b

11) He had been very ill and was now only a _____ of his former self.

12) The police raided the flat but it was _____ and the suspects had disappeared.

13) She was tired of _____ blamed for things that were not her fault.

14) "It's a _____ you aren't free, we would love to have you join us."

15) He had fallen a long way behind but there was _____ of time left to catch up.

16) The rabbit's fur was soft to the _____ and she stroked it affectionately.

17) They searched in vain for the key but it was a complete _____ of time.

18) The investigators looked for clues to the _____ of the rail crash.

19) She drove _____ the junction and had to turn around.

20) He is a handyman and does _____ jobs for people.

Score / 10

© 2006 Stephen Curran

Word Bank

copy, empty, taste, haste, pity, plenty, waste, goodbye

TOTAL 2,100

105

Across

1. Something that makes something happen.
3. Elapsed or gone by.
5. Feeling of sympathy for somebody else.
6. Unusual or peculiar.
10. Sense that identifies flavours.
11. Use something carelessly or without effect.
12. Stiffening substance for fabrics.
13. Vertical spar that supports sails, rigging or flags on a ship.
15. Existence.
16. Great speed.
19. For the reason that.

Down

1. One of many identical specimens.
2. Containing nothing.
4. Darkened shape of something.
7. An adequate or more than adequate amount.
8. Secure something or shut tightly.
9. Farewell.
14. Curved structure that forms the upper edge of an open space.
17. Feeling sense.
18. Happening immediately.

Mystery Letter

Score /20

© 2006 Stephen Curran

loss   lose   glory
history   manage   savage
package   postage   remind
respond   repent   record

Across

106

Down

1. To tell about what happened.
4. Organisation for maintaining law and order.
5. Violent, brutal, or undomesticated.
6. A piece cut from something.
10. To react.
12. The price paid for mail delivery.
14. What happened in the past.
16. The fame, admiration and honour given to somebody who does something important.
17. Join two pieces of rope by interweaving the strands of each into the other.
19. Send goods abroad.

1. To cause a person to remember or think of something or somebody else.
2. To achieve something with difficulty.
3. To make a lasting account of something.
7. To recognise the wrong in something you have done and to be sorry about it.
8. The number 40.
9. To put things into a container or wrappings.
11. An announcement of information.
13. The amount of money by which a company's expenses exceed income.
15. Fail to win.
18. Bring in from abroad.

Mystery Letter

Score

20

30

© 2006 Stephen Curran

slice splice
notice police
report import
export forty

Word Bank TOTAL 2,120

Exercise 106a

1) I bought some stamps to pay the _____ on a parcel that I sent to Newcastle.

2) *Ali Baba and the _____ Thieves* is a favourite children's story.

3) He was the Olympic Champion and revelled in the honour and the _____ .

4) "You will have to _____ me of the date: I have a terrible memory."

5) My company used to _____ its products all over the world.

6) We _____ many of the goods today that we used to manufacture ourselves.

7) I _____ to make ends meet with only a very small pension.

8) He reported the theft of his bike to the _____ .

9) The death of Sir Winston Churchill was a great _____ to the nation.

10) It was a _____ attack and he was very badly injured.

Score / 10

Exercise 106b

11) He promised to _____ and mend his ways.

12) It was a difficult question to which he was unsure how to _____ .

13) "He's showing off! Take no _____ of him."

14) "Would you like a _____ of buttered toast with marmalade?"

15) She used a courier company to deliver the _____ .

16) He was very angry but he tried to stay calm and not to _____ his temper.

17) It was a detailed _____ and left out none of the facts.

18) She set the video timer to _____ this week's episode of her favourite serial.

19) The projectionist managed to _____ together the two ends of the film.

20) He enjoyed learning about the past in _____ lessons.

Score / 10

© 2006 Stephen Curran

rheumatism **rhubarb** **tobacconist**
accordion **buccaneer** **confectioner**
stationer **detective** **ironmonger**
secretary **fruitier** **jeweller**

Exercise 107a

1) Her _____ worsened and her joints became stiffer.

2) A closed order of monks had lived in the _____ for over nine centuries.

3) Engineers were fitting new cables to the electricity _____ in the field.

4) "Would you like ice cream or custard with your _____ crumble?"

5) It is an old-fashioned _____ 's shop that sells sweets from a jar.

6) The _____ had just the right hinges that my Dad needed.

7) She is an excellent _____ with a nose for a good story.

8) Their wedding reception was held in a _____ in her parents' garden.

9) The National Trust restored the _____ and it can grind flour once again.

10) The London Millennium _____ housed an exhibition.   Score ▱ 10

Exercise 107b

11) The old man could no longer manage the stairs, so he bought a _____ .

12) "This new orange cordial tastes much _____ than the old one."

13) The old biplane was in the _____ undergoing a full restoration.

14) The _____ reset the diamond in her ring.

15) He plays the _____ for a group of morris dancers.

16) His _____ was ill and he had to type his own letters.

17) The _____ sold my Granddad a new pipe.

18) I like to read _____ stories and to work out who committed the crime.

19) Many a _____ preyed on ships in the West Indies in the 17th century.

20) She went to the _____ 's to buy a new fountain pen.   Score ▱ 10

Word Bank

journalist, pylon, hangar, bungalow, windmill, dome, marquee, monastery

TOTAL 2,140

107

Across

2. Maker or seller of sweets.
4. Somebody who investigates wrongdoing and gathers evidence.
5. Hemispherical roof.
6. A building with a set of wind-driven revolving sails or blades to drive a grinding machine.
10. Plant with green or pink leaf stalks that are edible when cooked.
12. Very large tent used for parties, meetings, sales and exhibitions.
14. A pirate.

Across (continued)

15. A seller of paper, envelopes, pens, pencils and other things used in writing.
16. Building housing aircraft.
17. Stiffness in joints and muscles.
18. Metal tower supporting high-voltage cables.
19. Someone who works as a writer or editor for a newspaper, magazine, or for radio or television.

Down

1. Someone who makes, sells or repairs jewellery.
3. Dealer in tools and other articles made chiefly of metal.
7. Person or shop that specialises in selling cigarettes, tobacco and pipes.
8. A monk's residence.
9. More reminiscent of fruit.
11. General clerical and administrative worker.
13. Air-driven musical instrument.
14. Single-storey house.

! Don't forget to go back to page **21** and complete **Kate's Mystery Word**.

Mystery Letter | Score / 20

© 2006 Stephen Curran

At the Dentist

Can you find all these words in the picture below? Write the correct word against each number. When you have finished you can colour in the picture if you want to.

chair	dental nurse	syringe	dentures	tissues
gloves	mouthwash	tooth	poster	x-ray
computer	basin	instruments	tunic	jacket

1. _____ 2. _____ 3. _____
4. _____ 5. _____ 6. _____
7. _____ 8. _____ 9. _____
10. _____ 11. _____ 12. _____
13. _____ 14. _____ 15. _____

34   © 2006 Stephen Curran

In the Accident & Emergency Department

Can you find all these words in the picture below? Write the correct word against each number.

chart	doctor	ambulance	cylinder	pills
stethoscope	curtain	blanket	bandage	form
patient	seat	monitor	mattress	trolley

1. _____ 2. _____ 3. _____
4. _____ 5. _____ 6. _____
7. _____ 8. _____ 9. _____
10. _____ 11. _____ 12. _____
13. _____ 14. _____ 15. _____

granary abattoir restaurant
cannibal announcer penniless
receipt conceited democracy
detergent eighty honesty

Exercise 108a

1) It had been a good harvest and the _____ was full.

2) She was born in 1920 and was _____ in the year 2000.

3) _____ falls around Whit Sunday: the seventh Sunday after Easter.

4) He is very _____ and has an excessively high belief in his own ability.

5) The _____ 's voice boomed out from the public address system.

6) "If you have the _____ for the purchase, I can exchange the goods."

7) My auntie plays cards at a _____ drive every Wednesday afternoon.

8) The space rocket's _____ increased rapidly as it climbed towards the stars.

9) Animals are taken to an _____ to be slaughtered humanely.

10) My Granddad drinks Scotch _____ with soda water.

Score ☐ / 10

Exercise 108b

11) All the tables in the _____ were full, so they had to eat elsewhere.

12) In a _____ people elect their representatives to govern them.

13) The _____ killed and ate the explorer.

14) The first time that you ride a bike it is a _____ but it soon becomes mundane.

15) She _____ 'goodnight' to her baby and quietly left the bedroom.

16) He returned the purse she dropped and she admired his _____ .

17) The tramp was _____ and kept his few possessions in a carrier bag.

18) The cat's _____ were covered with milk when it had finished drinking.

19) The frightened puppy began to _____ as he approached it.

20) They used a strong _____ to disperse the oil slick.

Score ☐ / 10

36 © 2006 Stephen Curran

Word Bank TOTAL 2,160

velocity
whist
Whitsuntide
whimper
novelty
whiskers
whisky
whispered

108

Across

1. Somebody who provides informative comment on something.
5. Truthfulness.
7. Alcoholic beverage made from fermented grain.
9. Sob softly.
12. Very poor or without any money.
14. Newness and originality.
16. The control of an organisation by all of its members.
17. The days around Whit Sunday.
18. Someone who eats human flesh.
19. A cleansing substance that dissolves dirt and oil.

Down

2. An eating place.
3. Hair growing near an animal's mouth.
4. A place where animals are slaughtered.
6. Eight times ten.
7. A card game that is the forerunner of bridge.
8. Spoke or suggested something in a confidential or furtive manner.
10. Acknowledgement that something has been received.
11. Grain warehouse.
13. Too proud.
15. Speed.

Put the mystery letters from the starred squares (*) in puzzles **108** to **115** into their numbered box below, then rearrange them to make **Oliver's Mystery Word**. The clue is **FUEL**.

Enter your mystery letters here:
108 109 110 111 112 113 114 115

Now rearrange them to make the:
Mystery Word:

© 2006 Stephen Curran

smoulder   boulder   athlete
rocket   clipper   motorcycle
peregrine hare   luggage
maggot   begging   leggings

Across

109

1. Slanting or oblique.
2. Large rock.
6. Protective covering for the lower leg.
9. Worm-shaped insect lava.
10. Leaves of a plant or tree.
11. Asking for something in a very intense, humble, or even humiliating way.
12. A competitor in track-and-field events.
13. Oval tissue mass in the back of the mouth, important for the body's immune system.

Across (continued)

14. A thin sheet of material with a cut-out design.
15. Large fast-running member of the rabbit family.
16. Fast mid-19th-century tall sailing ship.
17. Space vehicle.

Down

1. Springtime plant with yellow trumpet-shaped flowers.
3. Suitcases and bags used during a journey.
4. Long narrow sledge without runners.
5. A two-wheeled road vehicle powered by an engine.
6. Plant of the pea family with edible seeds.
7. Tool or container.
8. Coming from another region or country, wandering or travelling.
14. Burn slowly.

Mystery Letter

Score 20

38   © 2006 Stephen Curran

Word Bank

toboggan   tonsil
lentil   stencil
utensil   daffodil
foliage   diagonal

TOTAL 2,180

Exercise 109a

1) A _____ stopped, sat bolt-upright, listened with his large ears and then ran off.

2) A box junction is denoted by _____ yellow lines painted on the road.

3) He raced down the snow-covered hill on his _____ .

4) The _____ courier weaved his machine through the heavy traffic.

5) The Welsh celebrate St. David's day by wearing a _____ .

6) A huge _____ had fallen from the cliff and rolled across the promenade.

7) The _____ falcon's rapid downward stoop with closed wings is remarkable.

8) A colander is a kitchen _____ used to drain food cooked in water.

9) Orang-utans live and hide in the thick _____ of forest trees.

10) The bonfire continued to _____ for several hours.

Score / 10

Exercise 109b

11) A _____ is either of the two small oval tissue masses at the back of the mouth.

12) She asked a gentleman to lift her suitcase onto the _____ rack.

13) A _____ engine's thrust is produced by expelling expanding hot gases.

14) Chaps are protective leather _____ worn on horseback by cowboys.

15) He reeled in his fishing line and put a new fly _____ on the hook.

16) You must follow an intensive training regime to be a top track or field _____ .

17) They sprayed 'HANDLE WITH CARE' on the packing case using a _____ .

18) The orphaned children were _____ on the streets of Calcutta.

19) She made a tasty _____ soup that was rich in protein.

20) The *Cutty Sark* is perhaps the best known _____ .

Score / 10

© 2006 Stephen Curran

financial	valiant	diameter
civilians	dignified	satisfied
defied	crucified	magnified
hose	firemen	ambulance

Exercise 110a

1) She was very seriously ill but made a _____ recovery.

2) He connected the sprinkler to the _____ and watered the lawn.

3) The box contained a collection of _____ motorcycle parts.

4) They dialled 999 and an _____ arrived several minutes later.

5) Several _____ wearing breathing apparatus entered the burning building.

6) Many _____ were killed in air raids during the London Blitz.

7) He was very brave and made a _____ attempt to rescue the children.

8) My Mummy took me to the hospital's _____ department when I fell over.

9) Not _____ with only one sweet, the child took three more!

10) The plumber measured the _____ of the pipe.

Score /10

Exercise 110b

11) The Harrier jump jet _____ gravity and hovered five metres above the ground.

12) Running round and round the track became very boring and _____ .

13) The strand of human hair, _____ under the microscope, looked like string.

14) The Lords looked very _____ as their procession entered Parliament.

15) He recounted a very _____ anecdote and the audience laughed.

16) The jury all agreed and returned a _____ verdict.

17) For Halloween the children wore _____ masks of vampires and ghouls.

18) The _____ markets closed with the dollar weaker against the pound.

19) It was a _____ and nerve-racking moment as he prepared to bungee jump.

20) Jesus Christ was _____ on the cross at Calvary.

Score /10

40 © 2006 Stephen Curran

Word Bank

casualty, miraculous, unanimous, miscellaneous, tense, hideous, monotonous, humorous

TOTAL 2,200

110

Across

2. Executed by crucifixion.
4. Accident victim.
8. Vehicle for carrying people to and from hospital.
10. Challenged authority or power and refused to obey.
12. Increased the apparent size.
15. Flexible tube or pipe.
16. Composed of many varied things that have no necessary connection with each other.
17. Line through the centre of a circle.
18. Contented or pleased.

Down

1. Witty or funny.
3. Connected with money.
5. Worried or nervous and not relaxed.
6. Agreed on by everyone.
7. Horrible to see.
9. Totally unexpected, extraordinary, and marvellous.
11. Driver's assistant on a railway train.
12. Repetitious and uninteresting.
13. Ordinary citizens and not members of the armed forces.
14. Showing self-respect.

Mystery Letter

Score / 20

© 2006 Stephen Curran

41

anonymous   foremost   forecast
forearm   foreman   merciful
colourful   dreadful   tasteful
painful   painfully   dolefully

Across

4. Man in charge of other workers.
9. In a way that corresponds to fact or reality, or that expresses the truth.
11. Lower arm between the elbow and the wrist.
13. In a manner very pleasing to the senses.
14. Laboriously or embarrassingly badly.
17. Unnamed.
18. Producing great fear or awe.
19. Nearest to the front.
20. Very sadly and mournfully.

Down

1. Happily and optimistically.
2. Interesting and exciting.
3. Showing good aesthetic taste.
5. Great physical strength and energy.
6. Hurting as a result of an injury or disease.
7. A shape's outline.
8. Magnificence.
10. In a manner authorised or permitted by the law.
12. Showing compassion.
15. With a protective metal covering.
16. Predict what will happen.

Mystery Letter

Score 20

beautifully **cheerfully**
lawfully **truthfully**
vigour **splendour**
contour **armoured**

Word Bank TOTAL 2,220

Exercise 111a

1) It was an _____ letter without an address or signature.

2) The _____ security van collected the supermarket's daily takings.

3) He went to the dentist because he had a very _____ abscess under his tooth.

4) The flowers that they had planted made a very _____ display.

5) By studying the map's _____ lines, he knew that the hill was very steep.

6) The room was decorated _____ with gilded bosses on the ceiling.

7) The young shoots grew with _____ and soon needed to be cut back.

8) Rain was _____ for the weekend, so she cancelled the barbecue.

9) He made a _____ mistake which he regretted for the rest of his life.

10) The _____ gave instructions to the factory workers.

Score /10

Exercise 111b

11) He had always lived his life _____ and everyone was shocked by his crime.

12) The mourners at her funeral stood _____ at the graveside.

13) The interior of the Russian palace exuded opulence and _____ .

14) Our milkman seemed very happy and came up the path whistling _____ .

15) He stowed the crate towards the front in the _____ section of the hold.

16) The patients were treated by _____ and compassionate nuns.

17) The karate black belt used his _____ to parry the blow.

18) The decor is very _____ with velvet drapes and matching soft furnishings.

19) His knee was injured and he limped _____ off the pitch.

20) She was under oath and gave her evidence _____ .

Score /10

© 2006 Stephen Curran

appetite   **appalling**   **apprentice**
apparatus   **worrying**   **hurrying**
bullying   **copying**   **replying**
burying   **denying**   **pitying**

Exercise 112a

1) The rain continued to _____ and they had to stay indoors all day.

2) His business was expanding so he took on a young _____ to train.

3) Jack was always good at sport but he used to _____ at tennis.

4) "Pass the tomato _____ , I want to put some on my chips."

5) The _____ in the gymnasium was old and needed replacing.

6) The older boys were caught _____ and threatening the younger boys.

7) My dog is always digging holes and _____ things in the garden.

8) She opened the vacuum _____ and poured out a hot drink for each of them.

9) Everyone was _____ along the road so as not to be late for the match.

10) Children learn how to do things by _____ others.   **Score** /10

Exercise 112b

11) It was an _____ mess with twisted metal and broken glass everywhere.

12) His face showed he was angry and he continued to _____ at the boys.

13) Dick Fosbury developed the high jump technique known as the 'Fosbury _____ '.

14) "When _____ to the advertisement, please send two photographs."

15) If you eat snacks between meals you will spoil your _____ .

16) The strong breeze made the tall plane trees _____ gently to and fro.

17) "It's useless _____ that you were there, you were seen by three people."

18) He is always _____ about everything and never enjoys himself.

19) "Don't spend your time _____ somebody. Try to help them!"

20) It was a complete mystery and it continued to _____ her.   **Score** /10

44   © 2006 Stephen Curran

Word Bank

excel baffle
scowl flask
sway drizzle
flop ketchup

Word Bank TOTAL 2,240

Across

4. Thick savoury sauce, usually made with tomatoes, that is served cold as a condiment.
7. Digging a hole, putting something in it, and then replacing the soil.
8. Sit or lie down heavily.
10. A frown expressing anger, displeasure, or menace.
11. To swing back and forth.
14. Declaring that something is not true.
17. Making an identical version.
18. Dreadful or shocking.
19. Trainee learning an art, craft, or trade as a profession.

Down

1. Feeling sadness because somebody else is in trouble or pain.
2. Rushing.
3. Equipment used for a particular purpose.
5. Responding to what somebody says.
6. A small glass bottle.
7. Intimidating a weaker person.
9. Being or making anxious.
12. To do better than all others or than a given standard.
13. Light steady rain.
15. To puzzle somebody.
16. Natural desire for food.

112

Mystery Letter   Score /20

© 2006 Stephen Curran

45

planet   quintuplets   scotch
cider   jogging   oxygen
droop   squaw   scrabble
pounce   stray   bleach

Across

113

4. Alcoholic drink made from apples.
7. Colourless, odourless gas, necessary for combustion and animal respiration.
11. Animal's nose and jaws.
12. To jump suddenly onto something.
13. Running at a moderate pace as exercise.
16. Walking aids.
18. Whisky produced in Scotland.
19. Native North American woman or wife.
20. Close and reopen both eyes rapidly.

Down

1. To produce bubbles of gas.
2. Hang or bend down limply.
3. Five offspring borne to one mother from a single pregnancy.
5. Moving something rapidly to and fro.
6. Astronomical body orbiting a star.
8. Chemical substance that removes colour.
9. Almost asleep.
10. Shine with a flicker.
14. Grope about frantically in an effort to find something.
15. Enormous.
17. Wander away.

Mystery Letter

Score 20

© 2006 Stephen Curran

Word Bank

huge   twinkle
wagging   drowsy
fizz   crutches
muzzle   blink

Word Bank TOTAL 2,260

Exercise 113a

1) His rifle had just been discharged and its _____ was still smoking.

2) A fire needs three elements: fuel, heat and _____ .

3) He saw the North Star _____ in the cold night sky.

4) She had to _____ around on the floor to retrieve the dropped coins.

5) The company issued a press release to _____ rumours about its demise.

6) She accidentally splashed _____ on her blouse and it removed the colour.

7) She put her ear nearer to the glass and could hear the _____ of the lemonade.

8) She gave birth to _____ and they had to buy five of everything.

9) While his leg was in plaster, he got around on _____ .

10) Jupiter is the largest _____ in the solar system.

Score ____ / 10

Exercise 113b

11) He found an old book that referred to a Red Indian's wife as his _____ .

12) The friends go _____ together in the park in order to keep fit.

13) The West Country is renowned for producing _____ from pressed apples.

14) "Stay near me and don't _____ too far or we may lose each other."

15) The nurse told her to _____ rapidly to remove the grit from her eye.

16) He was very tired and began to feel _____ .

17) A _____ wave, over five metres tall, crashed over the ship's deck.

18) Her dog was very pleased to see her and was _____ its tail.

19) With a sudden _____ , the cat leapt onto its prey.

20) The flowers began to _____ through lack of water.

Score ____ / 10

© 2006 Stephen Curran

47

scooter   **hiss**   **florist**
plaice   **dandruff**   **screech**
twist   **sizzle**   **bigger**
scab   **tandoori**   **stride**

Exercise 114a

1) Long after the accident, her skin was still discoloured from all the _____ .

2) His mother bought him a new shampoo to try to prevent his _____ .

3) My father _____ the train at seven forty-five each weekday morning.

4) She ordered _____ chicken with rice at the local Indian restaurant.

5) He bought a _____ from the bookshop to read on the train.

6) She ordered a wreath for her friend's funeral from the local _____ .

7) "Mum wants cod, Dad wants skate and I'll have _____ from the chip shop."

8) Mandy's boyfriend rides a motor _____ and she rides pillion.

9) The class learnt their _____ tables by rote.

10) The bacon began to _____ noisily in the frying pan.

Score / 10

Exercise 114b

11) He badly grazed his knee when he fell off his bike and a large _____ formed.

12) "That's the _____ pig I've ever seen!"

13) All the items with that particular _____ number had to be rejected.

14) The lane continued to _____ and turn for several miles.

15) The steam engine came to a sudden stop with a loud _____ of brakes.

16) He continued to blow and the balloon got _____ .

17) It would have worried most people but Graham took it all in his _____ .

18) He could hear the _____ of escaping air and he knew that the tyre was punctured.

19) No _____ of money can ever buy you happiness.

20) "Mind your _____ when you get off the bus."

Score / 10

© 2006 Stephen Curran

Word Bank

amount, multiplication, step, bruising, fattest, batch, paperback, catches

TOTAL 2,280

114

Across

5. Thickest or widest.
7. Of greater size, number, or amount.
10. Make a sound like a continuous 's'.
11. Someone who owns or works in a shop that sells flowers.
13. A hissing and splattering sound typical of food frying.
14. Takes hold of something that is travelling through the air.
17. Two-wheeled child's toy.
18. A quantity or degree of something.

Down

1. Marinated then baked or cooked in a clay oven (tandoor).
2. Walk along briskly with long regular steps.
3. Arithmetic operation symbolised by 'x'.
4. The crust over a healing wound.
6. To make one end turn in the opposite direction to the other.
7. Discoloration of the skin surface.
8. Large, edible, flat-bodied seafish that has brown skin with red or orange spots.
9. A softcover book.
12. Dry scales of dead skin that are shed from the scalp.
15. A high pitched grating sound.
16. The amount of material produced in one operation.
17. A stage in a progression towards some goal or target.

Mystery Letter

Score /20

© 2006 Stephen Curran

pawn   circled   sunshine
cleanest   qualify   taller
comment   thatched   thirst
counts   saddest   sharpest

Exercise 115a

1) Her washing machine was not _____ properly, so she called an engineer.

2) They spent a relaxing week _____ along the canal on a narrowboat.

3) His height is 1.9 metres and William is _____ than all his classmates.

4) The chess player moved his _____ diagonally and took his opponent's knight.

5) The _____ on either side of the road filled with water during a monsoon.

6) The _____ General advises the government on English law.

7) The police chief did not reply when asked to _____ on the events.

8) Solar, tidal and wind power are some of the _____ energy sources.

9) After another breach in security, the airport procedures were found _____ .

10) The pack of hyenas _____ around the stricken zebra.

Score /10

Exercise 115b

11) It was very pleasant in the _____ but much cooler in the shade.

12) In my school, a lot of _____ was placed on sport and drama.

13) It was one of the _____ days of his life when his best friend emigrated.

14) In historical romantic novels, a woman's _____ tries to persuade her to marry him.

15) To quench her _____ she drank a large, cold glass of fresh orange juice.

16) As it got _____ it became impossible to read the map without a torch.

17) "Status _____ for nothing here: we judge everyone on their merit."

18) She was extremely sarcastic and critical with the _____ tongue imaginable.

19) It is a pretty village in which all the cottages have _____ roofs.

20) She was fourth in her heat but failed to _____ for the final.

Score /10

© 2006 Stephen Curran

Word Bank

cruising, darker, ditches, emphasis, wanting, suitor, attorney, working

Word Bank TOTAL 2,300

115

Across

4. Remark or observation.
6. Says numbers in order usually starting at one.
9. Unhappiest.
11. To become eligible for a position or privilege.
12. Most able to cut.
14. Chess piece of the lowest value.
15. Travelling by sea on a pleasure trip.
17. Not lighter.
18. Considerably higher.

Down

1. Special importance, significance, or stress.
2. Somebody legally empowered by a document to make decisions and act on behalf of somebody else.
3. Least dirty.
4. Drew a ring around.
5. A desire or need to drink liquid.
7. Not meeting expectations or requirements.
8. Somebody on whose behalf a case is brought to a law court.
10. Roofed with straw or rushes.
12. Direct sunlight.
13. Long narrow drainage channels dug in the ground.
16. Capable of being used or operated.

Don't forget to go back to page 37 and complete Oliver's Mystery Word.

Mystery Letter

Score /20

© 2006 Stephen Curran

51

Book Five Word List

abattoir	branches	cooler	easier
above	bravely	copper	easiest
accordion	breakfast	copy	easily
afraid	brighter	copying	Easter
afternoon	brightest	cork	eighty
afterwards	bruising	counts	eleven
alike	buccaneer	creeping	emphasis
aloud	build	crew	empty
ambulance	building	crucified	excel
amount	built	cruising	export
announcer	bullying	crutches	fasten
anonymous	bungalow	cuff	fattest
answer	burnt	cure	fence
appalling	burying	daffodil	fifteen
apparatus	butterfly	daisies	fifth
appetite	calf	daisy	fifty
apprentice	cannibal	dandruff	financial
arch	capture	darker	finer
armoured	casualty	darkness	finger
army	catches	deaf	finish
around	cattle	deed	fir
athlete	cause	deeper	firemen
attorney	chance	defend	fixed
axe	cheer	defied	fizz
baffle	cheerfully	democracy	flame
batch	chew	denying	flask
battle	chief	detective	flesh
beautifully	Christmas	detergent	flew
because	cider	diagonal	float
begging	circled	diameter	flock
being	civilians	dignified	flop
between	classes	dishes	florist
bigger	clay	ditches	flying
birth	cleanest	dolefully	foliage
birthday	cling	dome	forearm
bitter	clipper	dread	forecast
bleach	cloak	dreadful	foreman
blink	coal	drizzle	foremost
bloom	colourful	droop	forest
border	comment	drowsy	forty
bottle	conceited	dwell	forward
boulder	confectioner	dying	four
boxes	content	earn	fourteen
branch	contour	earth	fourth

52 © 2006 Stephen Curran

Book Five Word List

frame	jeweller	notice	rank
friend	jogging	novelty	rate
fruitier	journalist	odd	rattle
gift	ketchup	order	receipt
glasses	kettle	oxygen	record
glory	knee	package	remark
goodbye	kneel	paid	remind
grace	knife	painful	remove
granary	knives	painfully	repair
grandmother	knock	paperback	repeat
grey	knot	past	repent
grief	lawfully	pawn	replying
grind	leaves	peach	report
half	leggings	peaches	respond
halves	lemon	penniless	restaurant
hangar	lentil	pepper	rheumatism
hare	lilies	peregrine	rhubarb
haste	lily	person	roam
heaven	loaf	picture	roast
heavier	loaves	pint	rocket
heaviest	lose	pity	saddest
heavy	loss	pitying	safer
hideous	luggage	plaice	safest
hiding	lying	planet	satisfied
hiss	maggot	plenty	savage
history	magnified	poem	scab
honesty	mail	poet	scooter
hoping	manage	police	scotch
hose	manner	postage	scout
however	marquee	pounce	scowl
huge	mast	present	scrabble
humorous	matter	pretend	scrape
hundred	merciful	price	screech
hurry	merrily	prove	secretary
hurrying	miner	provide	serve
husband	miraculous	pure	shadow
illness	miscellaneous	pylon	sharpest
import	monastery	qualify	shelf
inches	monotonous	quickly	shining
indeed	motorcycle	quiet	should
instant	move	quintuplets	shout
invite	multiplication	rail	shy
ironmonger	muzzle	raise	silly
jail	nearly	raised	simple

© 2006 Stephen Curran

Book Five Word List

since	stiff	threw	vigour
sixteen	stray	thrown	visit
sixty	stride	tie	voice
sizzle	strike	tied	wagging
skate	strip	tired	wanting
skating	stuff	tobacconist	war
slice	sugar	toboggan	waste
slipped	suitor	toe	wheel
smiling	sunshine	together	whimper
smoulder	sure	tonsil	whiskers
snail	sway	touch	whisky
soak	swimming	towards	whispered
soap	taller	track	whist
sore	tandoori	trunk	Whitsuntide
space	taste	truthfully	windmill
spider	tasteful	trying	wise
splendour	tenth	twelve	wives
splice	term	twenty	wolf
spy	tense	twice	wool
squaw	thatched	twinkle	working
starch	themselves	twist	worrying
starve	thief	unanimous	worth
stationer	thieves	upset	wrap
steel	thirst	usual	write
steep	thirteen	utensil	writing
stencil	thirty	valiant	wrote
step	thousand	velocity	yesterday

Congratulations!

You have now learnt to spell **2,300** words, know what they mean and how to use them in a sentence.

Now move on to **Book 6** to learn lots more words to add to your word bank total.

Answers

11+ Spelling & Vocabulary
Workbook 5

Exercise 93a
1) skate
2) safer
3) grief
4) deeper
5) darkness
6) brightest
7) smiling
8) chief
9) hoping
10) hiding

Exercise 93b
11) shining
12) skating
13) brighter
14) finer
15) illness
16) safest
17) cooler
18) thief
19) miner
20) burnt

Crossword No. 93

Letter = N

Exercise 94a
1) Easter
2) poet
3) wrote
4) nearly
5) repeat
6) clay
7) should
8) repair
9) Christmas
10) remove

Exercise 94b
11) poem
12) quickly
13) write
14) prove
15) remark
16) writing
17) cheer
18) wrap
19) grey
20) move

Crossword No. 94

Letter = E

Exercise 95a
1) grandmother
2) breakfast
3) branch
4) yesterday
5) coal
6) peach
7) roast
8) around
9) usual
10) However

Exercise 95b
11) branches
12) afternoon
13) float
14) afraid
15) roam
16) aloud
17) above
18) peaches
19) cloak
20) alike

Crossword No. 95

Letter = T

© 2006 Stephen Curran

55

11+ Spelling & Vocabulary Workbook 5

Answers

Exercise 96a
1) stuff
2) glasses
3) husband
4) towards
5) forward
6) border
7) twice
8) fence
9) cuff
10) Copper

Exercise 96b
11) worth
12) together
13) afterwards
14) classes
15) inches
16) pepper
17) starve
18) since
19) order
20) price

Crossword No. 96

Letter = S

Exercise 97a
1) quiet
2) birth
3) dishes
4) provide
5) track
6) forest
7) friend
8) present
9) bitter
10) fir

Exercise 97b
11) birthday
12) stiff
13) pretend
14) lemon
15) sugar
16) visit
17) boxes
18) dwell
19) silly
20) Hurry

Crossword No. 97

Letter = H

Exercise 98a
1) fourth
2) eleven
3) strip
4) simple
5) wool
6) fifth
7) serve
8) hundred
9) upset
10) tenth

Exercise 98b
11) term
12) cling
13) finger
14) flesh
15) gift
16) pint
17) person
18) four
19) bloom
20) twelve

Crossword No. 98

Letter = T

© 2006 Stephen Curran

Answers

11+ Spelling & Vocabulary Workbook 5

Exercise 99a
1) steep
2) space
3) soak
4) spider
5) wheel
6) earth
7) lily
8) bravely
9) chance
10) deed

Exercise 99b
11) steel
12) voice
13) earn
14) wise
15) invite
16) soap
17) daisy
18) daisies
19) lilies
20) grace

Crossword No. 99

Letter = C

Exercise 100a
1) Thirty
2) twenty
3) thousand
4) loaves
5) between
6) halves
7) thieves
8) fifteen
9) creeping
10) sixty

Exercise 100b
11) thirteen
12) sixteen
13) loaf
14) calf
15) fifty
16) shelf
17) fourteen
18) leaves
19) half
20) indeed

Crossword No. 100

Letter = U

Exercise 101a
1) knot
2) themselves
3) fixed
4) flew
5) thrown
6) knives
7) crew
8) chew
9) wolf
10) jail

Exercise 101b
11) snail
12) wives
13) mail
14) knock
15) kneel
16) knee
17) threw
18) rail
19) knife
20) grind

Crossword No. 101

Letter = I

In the Living Room
1. VASE
2. BOOKCASE
3. PEN
4. MAGAZINE
5. HEARTH
6. PLANT
7. SETTEE
8. CUSHION
9. SPEAKER
10. NEWSPAPER
11. PLUG
12. TELEVISION
13. MANTELPIECE
14. CANDLE
15. ARMCHAIR

In the Bathroom
1. TOILET
2. WATER
3. SOAP
4. SHOWER GEL
5. SHOWER
6. PEDESTAL
7. TOOTHBRUSH
8. WASH BASIN
9. MAT
10. TOOTHPASTE
11. TOWEL
12. RAZOR
13. CISTERN
14. TAPS
15. SCALES

© 2006 Stephen Curran

11+ Spelling & Vocabulary Workbook 5

Answers

Exercise 102a
1) dying
2) strike
3) picture
4) deaf
5) raise
6) finish
7) paid
8) sure
9) raised
10) cure

Exercise 102b
11) heaven
12) capture
13) trunk
14) dread
15) lying
16) flock
17) tie
18) pure
19) defend
20) tied

Crossword No. 102

Letter = C

Exercise 103a
1) kettle
2) swimming
3) battle
4) rate
5) manner
6) rattle
7) built
8) frame
9) matter
10) cattle

Exercise 103b
11) scrape
12) bottle
13) building
14) content
15) slipped
16) sore
17) flame
18) cork
19) tired
20) build

Crossword No. 103

Letter = T

Exercise 104a
1) easier
2) butterfly
3) heavy
4) trying
5) shy
6) axe
7) easiest
8) flying
9) heaviest
10) spy

Exercise 104b
11) heavier
12) rank
13) toe
14) shout
15) merrily
16) War
17) easily
18) army
19) Scout
20) answer

Crossword No. 104

Letter = R

58 © 2006 Stephen Curran

Answers

11+ Spelling & Vocabulary
Workbook 5

Exercise 105a
1) mast
2) instant
3) goodbye
4) copy
5) fasten
6) starch
7) taste
8) arch
9) because
10) haste

Exercise 105b
11) shadow
12) empty
13) being
14) pity
15) plenty
16) touch
17) waste
18) cause
19) past
20) odd

Exercise 106a
1) postage
2) Forty
3) glory
4) remind
5) export
6) import
7) manage
8) police
9) loss
10) savage

Exercise 106b
11) repent
12) respond
13) notice
14) slice
15) package
16) lose
17) report
18) record
19) splice
20) history

Exercise 107a
1) rheumatism
2) monastery
3) pylon
4) rhubarb
5) confectioner
6) ironmonger
7) journalist
8) marquee
9) windmill
10) Dome

Exercise 107b
11) bungalow
12) fruitier
13) hangar
14) jeweller
15) accordion
16) secretary
17) tobacconist
18) detective
19) buccaneer
20) stationer

Crossword No. 105

Letter = P

Crossword No. 106

Letter = O

Crossword No. 107

Letter = A

At the Dentist

1. JACKET	2. INSTRUMENTS	3. TISSUES	4. TUNIC	5. X-RAY
6. COMPUTER	7. TOOTH	8. SYRINGE	9. GLOVES	10. POSTER
11. DENTAL NURSE	12. CHAIR	13. MOUTHWASH	14. BASIN	15. DENTURES

In the Accident & Emergency Department

1. STETHOSCOPE	2. AMBULANCE	3. PATIENT	4. PILLS	5. MONITOR
6. CHART	7. SEAT	8. DOCTOR	9. CURTAIN	10. CYLINDER
11. BLANKET	12. BANDAGE	13. TROLLEY	14. FORM	15. MATTRESS

© 2006 Stephen Curran

11+ Spelling & Vocabulary Workbook 5

Answers

Exercise 108a
1) granary
2) eighty
3) Whitsuntide
4) conceited
5) announcer
6) receipt
7) whist
8) velocity
9) abattoir
10) whisky

Exercise 108b
11) restaurant
12) democracy
13) cannibal
14) novelty
15) whispered
16) honesty
17) penniless
18) whiskers
19) whimper
20) detergent

Crossword No. 108

Letter = I

Exercise 109a
1) hare
2) diagonal
3) toboggan
4) motorcycle
5) daffodil
6) boulder
7) peregrine
8) utensil
9) foliage
10) smoulder

Exercise 109b
11) tonsil
12) luggage
13) rocket
14) leggings
15) maggot
16) athlete
17) stencil
18) begging
19) lentil
20) clipper

Crossword No. 109

Letter = A

Exercise 110a
1) miraculous
2) hose
3) miscellaneous
4) ambulance
5) firemen
6) civilians
7) valiant
8) casualty
9) satisfied
10) diameter

Exercise 110b
11) defied
12) monotonous
13) magnified
14) dignified
15) humorous
16) unanimous
17) hideous
18) financial
19) tense
20) crucified

Crossword No. 110

Letter = F

© 2006 Stephen Curran

Answers

11+ Spelling & Vocabulary Workbook 5

Exercise 111a
1) anonymous
2) armoured
3) painful
4) colourful
5) contour
6) beautiful
7) vigour
8) forecast
9) dreadful
10) foreman

Exercise 111b
11) lawfully
12) dolefully
13) splendour
14) cheerfully
15) foremost
16) merciful
17) forearm
18) tasteful
19) painfully
20) truthfully

Crossword No. 111

Letter = R

Exercise 112a
1) drizzle
2) apprentice
3) excel
4) ketchup
5) apparatus
6) bullying
7) burying
8) flask
9) hurrying
10) copying

Exercise 112b
11) appalling
12) scowl
13) flop
14) replying
15) appetite
16) sway
17) denying
18) worrying
19) pitying
20) baffle

Crossword No. 112

Letter = P

Exercise 113a
1) muzzle
2) oxygen
3) twinkle
4) scrabble
5) scotch
6) bleach
7) fizz
8) quintuplets
9) crutches
10) planet

Exercise 113b
11) squaw
12) jogging
13) cider
14) stray
15) blink
16) drowsy
17) huge
18) wagging
19) pounce
20) droop

Crossword No. 113

Letter = N

© 2006 Stephen Curran

11+ Spelling & Vocabulary Workbook 5

Answers

Exercise 114a
1) bruising
2) dandruff
3) catches
4) tandoori
5) paperback
6) florist
7) plaice
8) scooter
9) multiplication
10) sizzle

Exercise 114b
11) scab
12) fattest
13) batch
14) twist
15) screech
16) bigger
17) stride
18) hiss
19) amount
20) step

Crossword No. 114

Letter = F

Exercise 115a
1) working
2) cruising
3) taller
4) pawn
5) ditches
6) Attorney
7) comment
8) cleanest
9) wanting
10) circled

Exercise 115b
11) sunshine
12) emphasis
13) saddest
14) suitor
15) thirst
16) darker
17) counts
18) sharpest
19) thatched
20) qualify

Crossword No. 115

Letter = A

Mystery Word
N E T S H T C U
C H E S T N U T

Mystery Word
I C T R P O A
A P R I C O T

Mystery Word
I A F R P N F A
P A R A F F I N

62

© 2006 Stephen Curran

PROGRESS CHARTS

Scores

(Grid: y-axis 1–20, x-axis 93–115)

Exercises

Shade in your score for each exercise on the graph. Add them up for your total score out of 460. Ask an adult to work out the percentage.

Total Score

Percentage

% A

Scores

(Grid: y-axis 1–20, x-axis 93–115)

Crosswords

Shade in your score for each crossword on the graph. Add them up for your total score out of 460.

Total Score

Percentage

% B

For the average percentage add %A and %B and divide by 2

Overall Percentage

%

© 2006 Stephen Curran

CERTIFICATE OF ACHIEVEMENT

This certifies

_____

has successfully completed

11+ Spelling & Vocabulary

WORKBOOK 5

Overall percentage score achieved [ ] %

Comment _____
_____

Signed _____
(teacher/parent/guardian)

Date _____